That Sinking Feeling

Adapted by
Geoffrey T. Williams

Illustrated by
Mark Marderosian
Jim Mitchell
Phil Ortiz
Jim Story
Kay Story
Don Williams

MALLARD
PRESS

Twin Books

The lights of St. Canard glowed like small fires in the
midnight sky. As an oil tanker slowly steamed toward the
Audubon Bay Bridge, its wake rippled in the black water
like a long snake.

Suddenly a huge column of water surged up, lifting the ship
a hundred feet into the air! Then, just as suddenly, the column
collapsed, and the ship dropped into a gaping hole in the river.
Water rushed in to fill the hole, and the tanker disappeared.

In another part of the city, music was blasting from the tallest
tower in the city as radio station KDUQ played St. Canard's rock
and roll favorites. At the top of the tower, a bright red light
cheerfully blinked on and off.

Abruptly, the tower began to shudder. Then it collapsed into a huge hole. The cheerful red light was the last thing to disappear.

Thousands of radios in the city were filled with the sound of a strange and ghostly silence.

The following morning, in a quiet suburban bedroom, Gosalyn Mallard grabbed the glass bowl on the bedside table and emptied it, goldfish and all, over her father's head.

"Wake up, Dad!" she shouted. "We have a case!"

Lurching up from the bed, Drake Mallard groaned. "Gosalyn! I'm gonna get . . . goo . . . glub . . ."

Drake spit the flip-flopping fish out of his beak. Then, grumbling about the lack of respect shown by nine-year-old daughters, he heaved himself out of bed.

When Drake strolled downstairs, he found Launchpad McQuack, Gosalyn and Honker Muddlefoot, Gosalyn's best friend, with their eyes glued to the television set.

"The disappearances of the *S.S. Langdale* and the KDUQ tower were not isolated events," the reporter announced. "One hour ago, the St. Canard Electric Plant sank out of sight in front of hundreds of frightened employees!"

"Yes," Drake Mallard said, "this is definitely a job for Darkwing Duck. Once again, I must come to the rescue of St. Canard. "It's a good thing you woke me, Gosalyn," he added.

Gosalyn and Honker ran out of the room, only to reappear almost immediately, dressed in mining hats and carrying ropes and pickaxes.

"We're ready to go, Dad!" she piped up.

"*We* are going nowhere, young lady," Drake answered. "You and Honker are going to be safely watching a ball game at the stadium while Launchpad and I mop up this mess!"

"But, Dad . . ." Gosalyn objected.

"No 'buts'," he said. "This is just one more misguided mischief-maker with another take-over-the-world scheme. We'll probably be back in time for dinner.

"Come on, Launchpad. Let's get dangerous!"

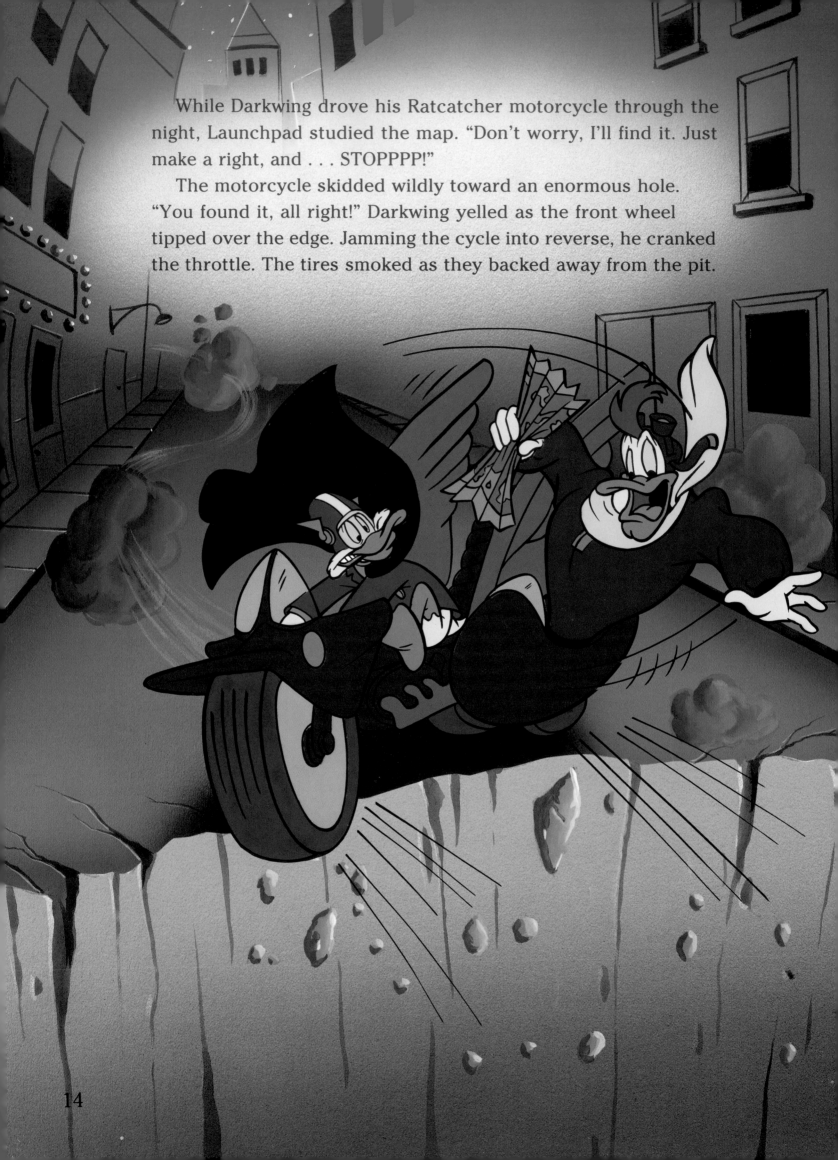

While Darkwing drove his Ratcatcher motorcycle through the night, Launchpad studied the map. "Don't worry, I'll find it. Just make a right, and . . . STOPPPP!"

The motorcycle skidded wildly toward an enormous hole. "You found it, all right!" Darkwing yelled as the front wheel tipped over the edge. Jamming the cycle into reverse, he cranked the throttle. The tires smoked as they backed away from the pit.

"Well," said Launchpad, "at least we know where the electric plant went. But how are we going to find it?"

"Ah-ha!" grinned Darkwing. "I have just the thing!" He uncoiled a long rope and began his descent. "Trust me!"

"I was afraid you'd say that," Launchpad sighed.

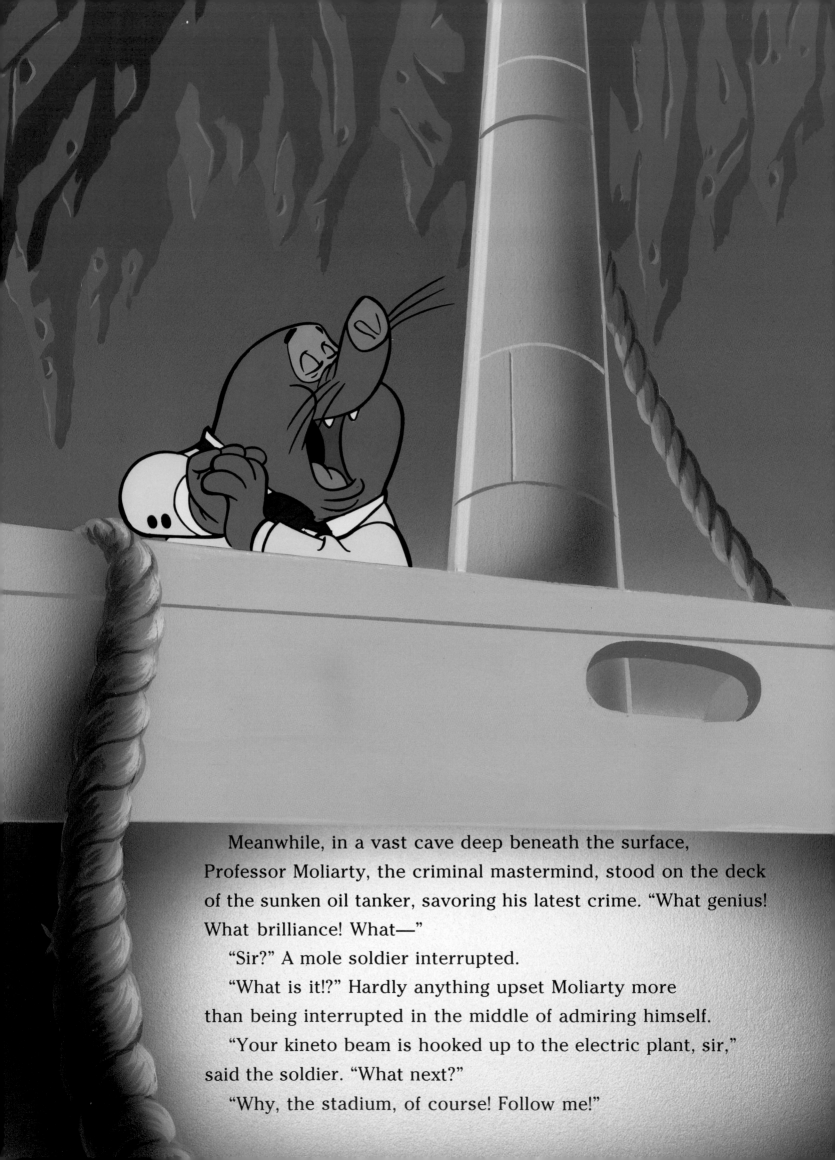

Meanwhile, in a vast cave deep beneath the surface, Professor Moliarty, the criminal mastermind, stood on the deck of the sunken oil tanker, savoring his latest crime. "What genius! What brilliance! What—"

"Sir?" A mole soldier interrupted.

"What is it!?" Hardly anything upset Moliarty more than being interrupted in the middle of admiring himself.

"Your kineto beam is hooked up to the electric plant, sir," said the soldier. "What next?"

"Why, the stadium, of course! Follow me!"

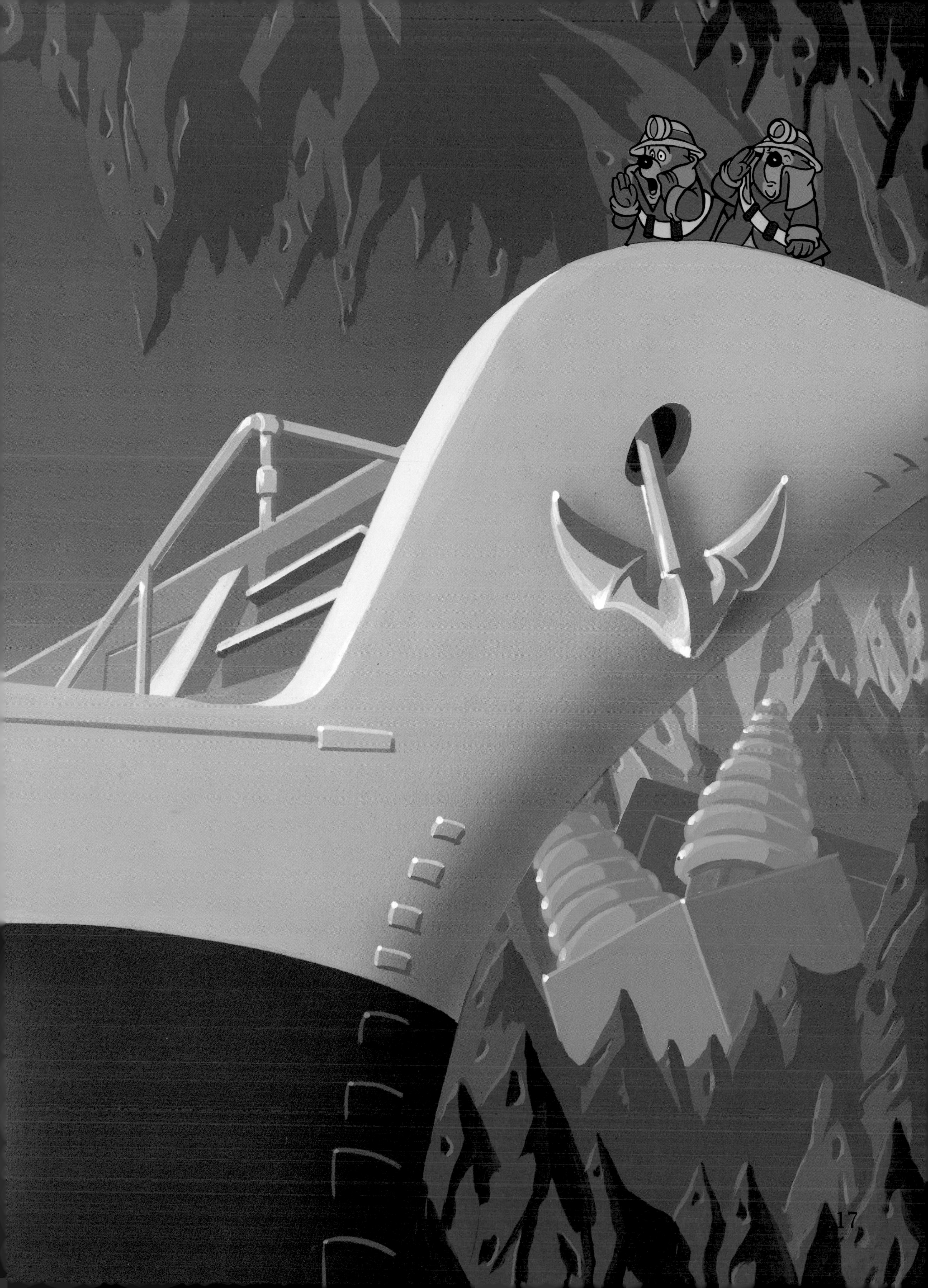

Moliarty hopped off the tanker deck. "My destiny is to lead you to your destiny!" he proclaimed to the moles. "And your destiny lies above, on the surface!"

"Boy, that's one mad mole," whispered Launchpad from behind a rock. "I don't like the look of him."

"I don't like the look of his machine," murmured Darkwing.

"It's too bright for us up there!" a mole soldier pointed out.
"Not for long!" shouted Moliarty, pulling a lever on the
machine. Giant gears and wheels shuddered into motion.
"Let the Age of Moles begin!" The ground shook and a
towering steel shaft began to lower.

Up above, Gosalyn and Honker were eating hot dogs and enjoying the ball game when the stadium started to sink.

"Come on, Gosalyn!" Honker yelled, bolting from his seat. "We've got to get out of here!" When he turned back, he saw that his friend was sinking with the stadium.

"I'm staying!" Gosalyn cried. "There's no way I'm going to miss this adventure!"

Scared as he was, Honker couldn't leave his best friend. "Here I come!" he cried, and holding his breath, he jumped back onto the stadium as it sank into the ground.

Under the stadium, Professor Moliarty leaped back as a massive boulder slammed into the machine, jamming the gears. The shaft screeched to a stop.

Moliarty was horrified. "My machine! What happened to my beautiful machine?"

Suddenly the sound of laughter echoed through the cave.

"Is that someone laughing at me?" Moliarty gasped. "I can't stand it! Who are you?"

"I am the terror that flaps in the night!" a voice called. "I am the winged scourge that pecks at your nightmares!" From a cloud of smoke on top of a rock, Darkwing emerged, swirling his cape.

"I am Darkwing Duck!"

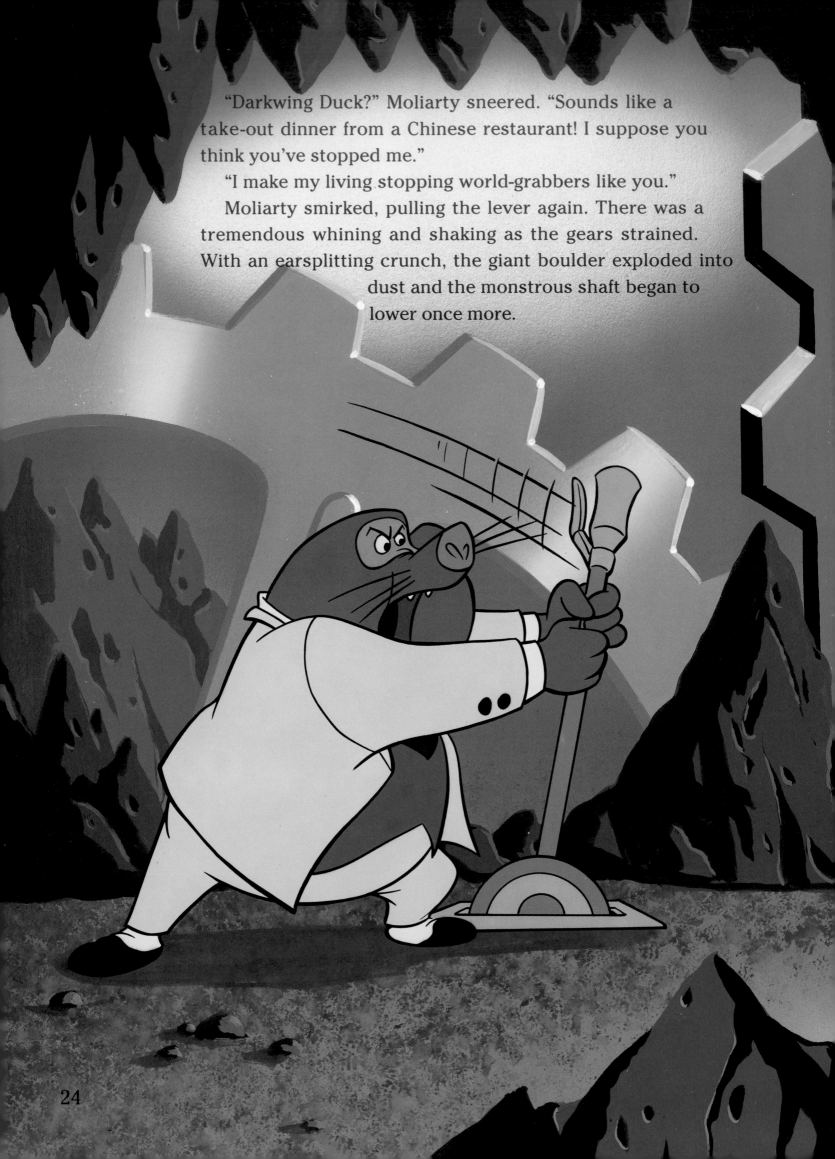

"Darkwing Duck?" Moliarty sneered. "Sounds like a take-out dinner from a Chinese restaurant! I suppose you think you've stopped me."

"I make my living stopping world-grabbers like you." Moliarty smirked, pulling the lever again. There was a tremendous whining and shaking as the gears strained. With an earsplitting crunch, the giant boulder exploded into dust and the monstrous shaft began to lower once more.

"Now who has stopped whom, Dinkwing Dupe?"
"Uh, that's 'Darkwing Duck'," Launchpad pointed out.

When the huge stadium came to rest, Gosalyn and Honker peeked over a ledge and saw Darkwing and Launchpad in the middle of a menacing mass of moles.

"What are we going to do, Honker?" Gosalyn whispered.

Doing some fast figuring on his calculator, Honker suggested, "Let's use the trash can to throw them off balance."

"Super idea! We'll trash the bad guys!" agreed Gosalyn.

They rolled the can down the ledge, intending to bowl down the moles so Darkwing and Launchpad could escape. Instead, the can bounced straight up in the air and came down on top of Darkwing and Launchpad! They were trapped!

"Oops!" whispered Honker. "I knew I should have checked the trajectory and terminal velocity."

Moliarty had Darkwing and Launchpad tied to a stake in the middle of a deep pit.

"Do you really think you can stop me—Darkwing Duck—with mere ropes?" laughed the terror that flaps in the night. "I expected a little more imagination from you, Moliarty."

Moliarty smiled an evil smile. "You mean something like giant slugs that suck the meat from your bones while they slime you to death?"

"That would be a start, I guess," gulped Darkwing.

"My poor darlings haven't eaten in such a long time," Moliarty said. "I imagine they'll be here in just a . . . why, yes! Here they come now! Ta-ta. I'm off to conquer the world."

The radio tower now jutted up from the middle of the stadium, forming a gigantic dish antenna. With oil from the tanker and electricity from the electric plant for power, the kineto beam was ready. The steel shaft hoisted the antenna to the surface.

Moliarty rubbed his hands together. "If the light of the surface world is too strong for moles, then I'll just have to turn it off! Activate the beam!"

The antenna turned until it pointed directly at the moon.
A bright beam of light shot out, and the moon began to move
across the sky. When it stopped, it completely covered the sun.
St. Canard was plunged into darkness!

"Behold! The first mole-made eclipse!" crowed Moliarty.

While the army of conquering moles advanced on the unsuspecting city above, Launchpad lamented, "Of all the ways to die, I have to go as slug bait!" From the blackness below, shiny bug eyes twitched on the ends of stalks as the giant slugs oozed their way toward the two prisoners.

Suddenly a voice at the edge of the pit shouted, "Dad!"

"Gosalyn?" gasped Darkwing. "Gosalyn! Is that you?"

"Yeah! And don't worry! Honker has everything figured out!"
She turned anxiously to Honker, who was calculating furiously.
"Honker, I think you'd better hurry!"

"But I've only rechecked my figures twice!"

The slugs slithered closer. "Honker!!" yelled the prisoners.

Grabbing his rifle, Honker fired. The bullet slammed into one rock column, then another.

Whack! Wham! The falling columns smashed the slugs, pitching them down to the bottom of the pit and forming a bridge to the prisoners.

"Aw-*right!* Way to go, Honker!" Gosalyn cheered, rushing across the bridge to untie Darkwing and Launchpad.

Launchpad grinned. "I knew you could do it, buddy," he said to Honker.

"Kid, I promise to buy you a faster calculator," said Darkwing, "but right now there's trouble up above." His eycs glinted as he swirled his cape.

"Let's get dangerous!"

St. Canard was in chaos!

Mole soldiers were everywhere, marching through the streets like a conquering army. Giant pill bugs from Moliarty's underground kingdom rumbled between skyscrapers like armored cars, bullets ricocheting off their shells. Giant slugs slimed over tanks as though they were toys!

How could an army like this be defeated?

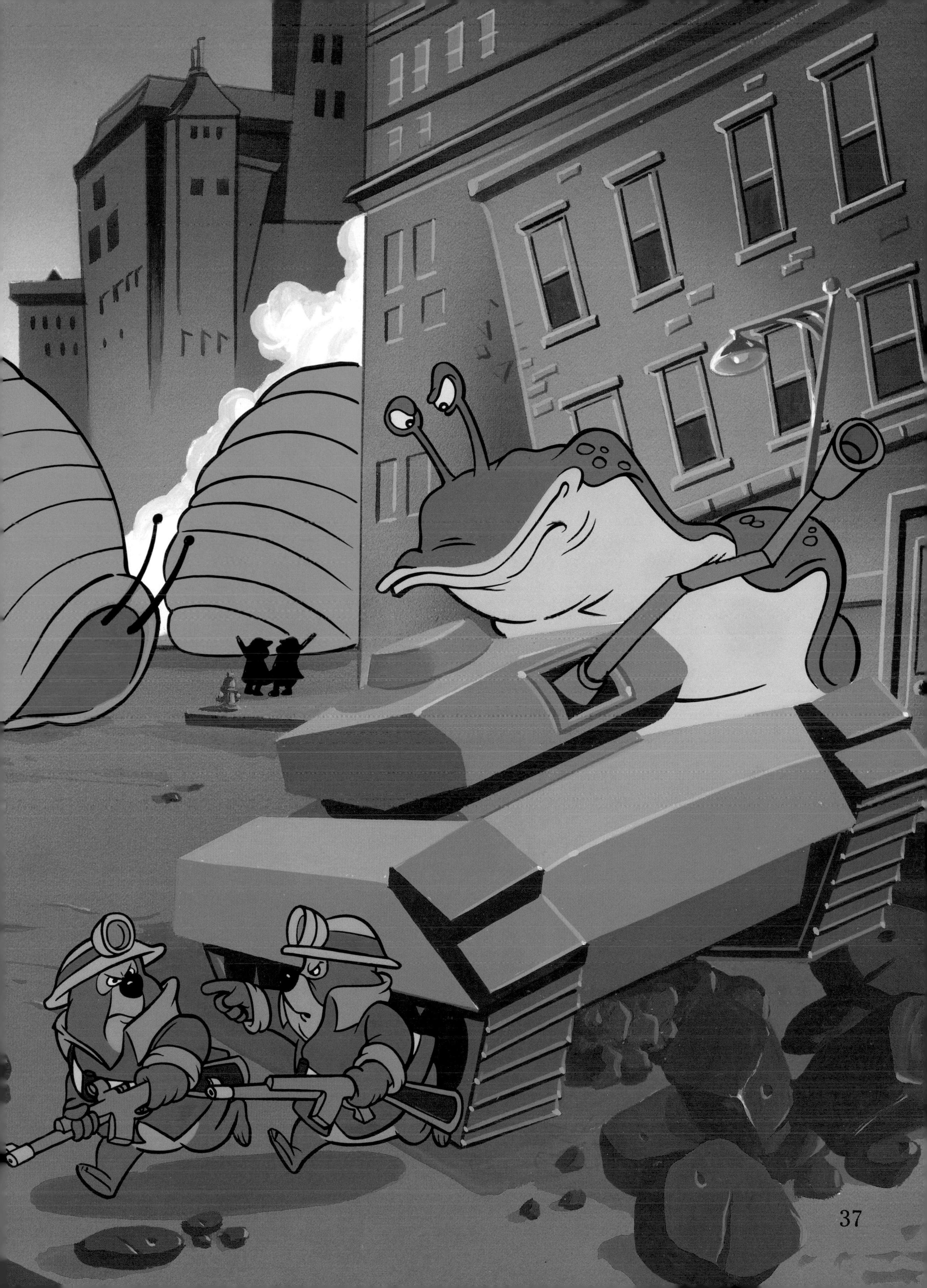

Darkwing Duck quickly surveyed the pandemonium as he and his companions burst out of the cavern.

"We have to cut the power to that kineto beam!" he shouted. Pulling out a small microphone, he whispered, "Darkwing Duck to Ratcatcher. Let's get dangerous!"

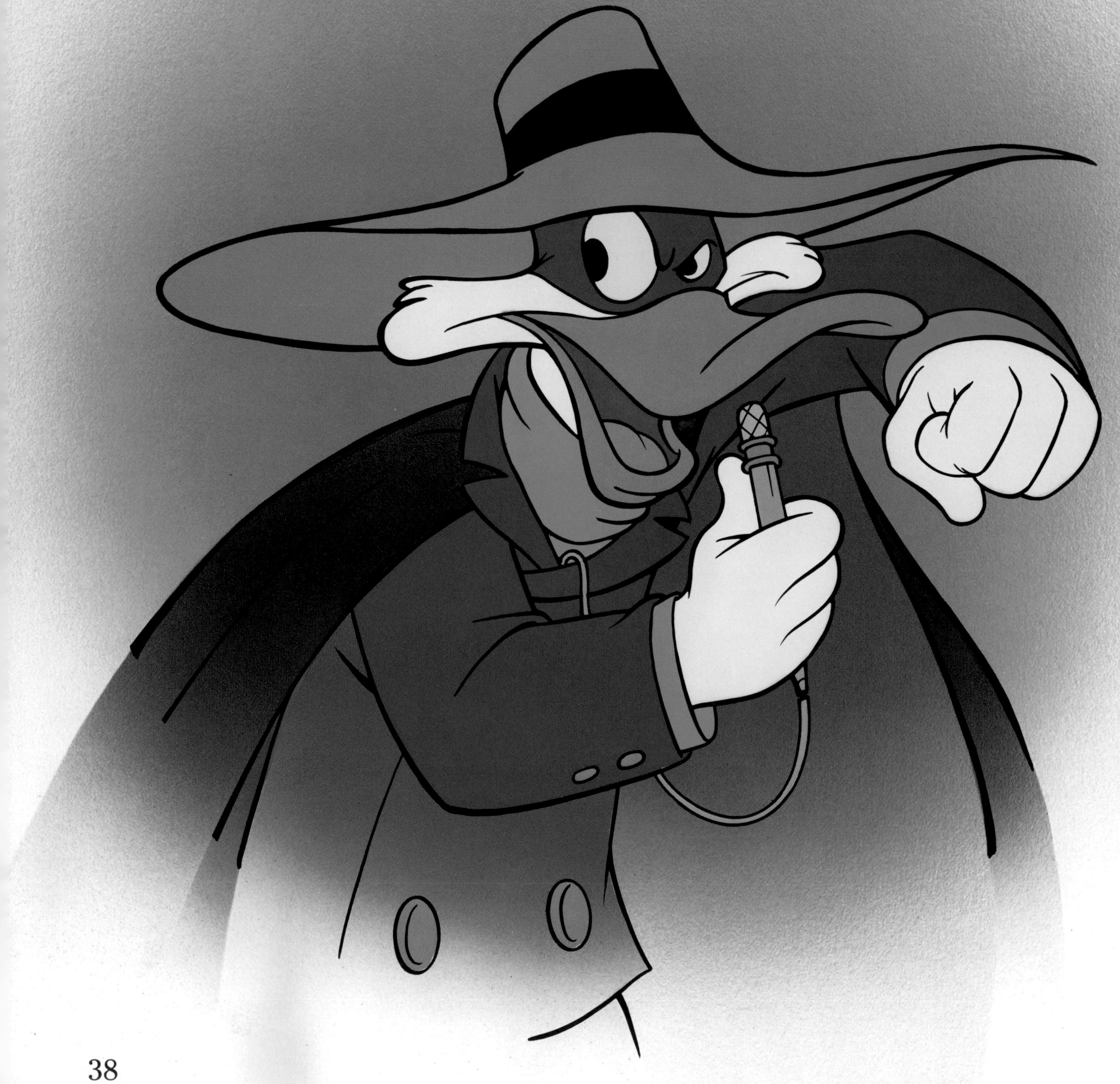

Several blocks away, the powerful motorcycle roared to life and homed in on Darkwing's signal.

Moments later, Darkwing and the others were zooming through the besieged city, dodging bullets and swerving around burning cars. Only one thing stood in their way.

"Look!" screamed Gosalyn.

On top of the stadium, Professor Moliarty was munching
on a foot-long hot dog and watching the Ratcatcher screech to a
halt. "That Dinkwing Dunce thinks he can get past my pill bug!
Imagine, matching wits with me!"

“Time for a little solo action,” Darkwing warned the others.

“Dad!” Gosalyn cried. “Please be careful!”

“Don’t worry, sweetheart,” he said, unhooking the cycle’s sidecar. “There’s not a mole made that can mess with me!” Then, revving the Ratcatcher’s engine until it screamed like a banshee, the world’s most fearless duck took off after the world’s biggest pill bug!

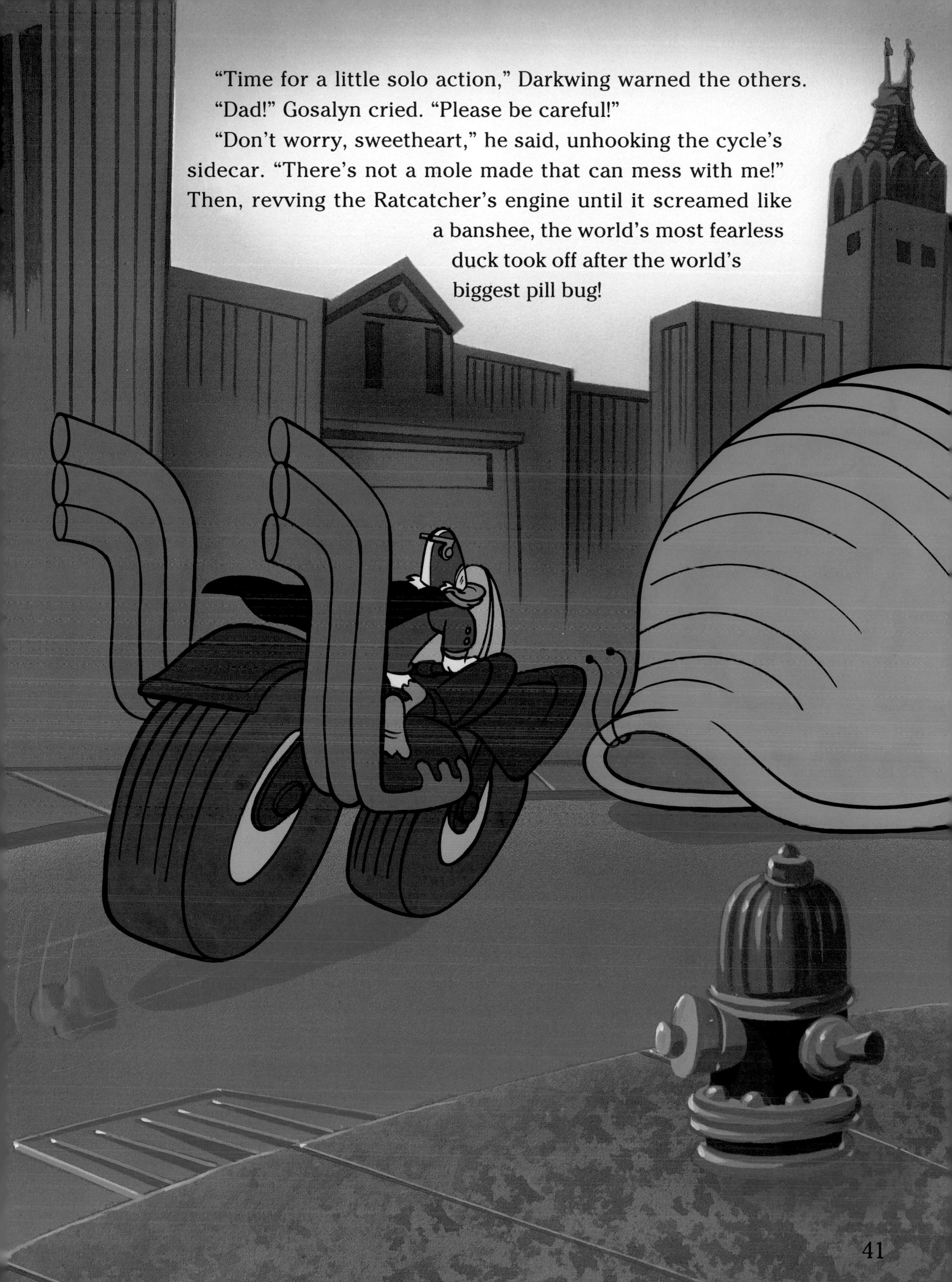

His cape flying in the wind, Darkwing yelled, "Okay, Ratcatcher! Show 'em what you can do!"

Just before bike met bug head-on, Darkwing popped a wheelie! The Ratcatcher soared up the steep slope of the pill bug's shell and sailed over the top of the stadium wall, heading for the giant antenna!

"NOOO!!" howled an enraged Moliarty.
Seconds later, Darkwing Duck slammed into the kineto-
beam antenna with a clang heard across the city.

Slowly, very slowly, the kineto beam began to tilt. The moon slid aside until, a few minutes later, bright sunlight once again blazed down on St. Canard!

Thousands of stunned mole soldiers, unable to bear the light of the sun, covered their eyes and groped their way back to their underground home. Pill bugs curled up and rolled after them. Slugs shriveled up on the streets like dried worms.

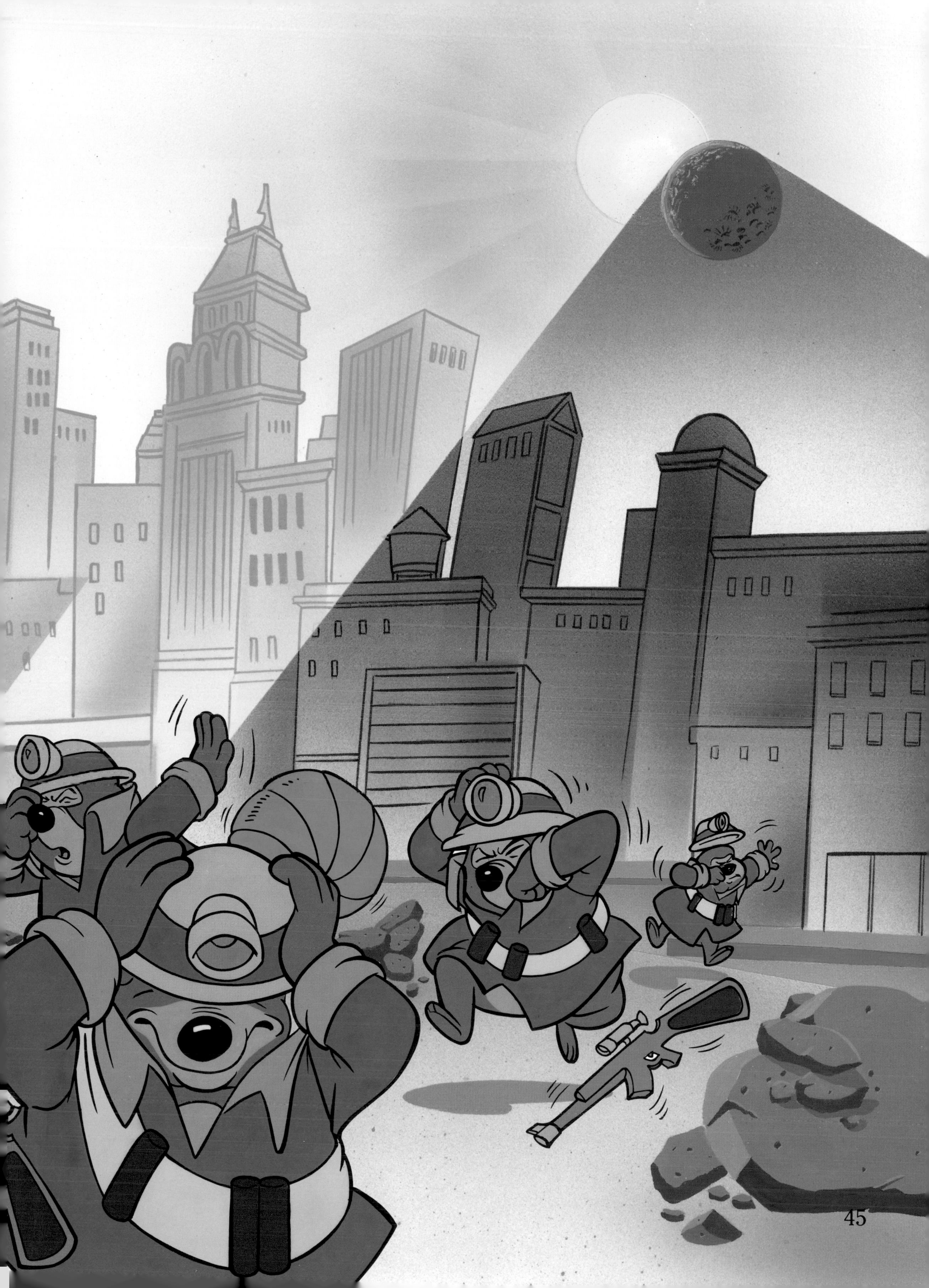

Professor Moliarty was almost insane with rage. "I'll get you for this, you foul-feathered fowl!" he screamed as he tunnelled his way back underground. "You haven't heard the last of me, Duncewing Dorp!"

"Uh, that's 'Darkwing Duck'!" Launchpad called after him.

"He knows, Launchpad. He knows," laughed Darkwing, hugging Gosalyn and Honker tightly.